A STRONG ROD BROKEN AND WITHERED

A STRONG ROD BROKEN AND WITHERED

A sermon preached at *Northampton,* on the Lord's Day, June 26th, 1748. On the death of The Honourable John Stoddard, Esq.

JONATHAN EDWARDS, A.M.

Pastor of the Church of CHRIST in *Northampton.*

And all the inhabitants of the earth are reputed as nothing: and he doeth according to his will in the army of heaven, and among the inhabitants of the earth: and none can stay his hand, or say unto him, What doest thou?—DANIEL 4:35.

CURIOSMITH

MINNEAPOLIS

Published by Curiosmith.
P. O. Box 390293, Minneapolis, Minnesota, 55439.
Internet: curiosmith.com.
E-mail: shopkeeper@curiosmith.com.

Previously—Boston: Printed by ROGERS and FOWLE for J. Edwards in
Cornhill, 1748.

The text of this edition is from *Works of Jonathan Edwards,* edited by Edward
Hickman, 1843.

The "Outline of the Contents" was added to this edition by the publisher.

ISBN 9781935626817

OUTLINE OF THE CONTENTS

—∘o❊❦❊o∘—

A STRONG
ROD BROKEN
AND WITHERED[1]

A SERMON BY

JONATHAN EDWARDS, A.M.

Her strong rods were broken and withered.
—EZEKIEL 19:12.

IN order to a right understanding and improvement of these words, these four things must be observed concerning them.

1. Who she is that is here represented as having had strong rods, *viz.* the Jewish community, who here, as often elsewhere, is called the people's mother. She is here compared to a vine planted in a very fruitful soil, verse 10 [Ezekiel 19]. The Jewish church and state is

1 God's Awful Judgment in the Breaking and Withering of the Strong Rods of a Community, preached at Northampton on the Lord's day, June 26, 1748, on the death of the Honourable John Stoddard, Esq. often a member of his Majesty's council, for many years chief justice of the court of Common Pleas for the county of Hampshire, judge of the probate of wills, and chief colonel of the regiment, etc. who died at Boston, June 19, 1748 in the 67th year of his age.

often elsewhere compared to a vine; as Psalm
80:8, etc. Isaiah 5:2; Jeremiah 2:21; Ezekiel 15
and chapter 17:6.

2. What is meant by her strong rods, *viz.* her
wise, able, and well qualified magistrates or rulers. That the rulers or magistrates are intended
is manifest by verse 11 [Ezekiel 19], "And she
had strong rods for the sceptres of them that
bear rule." And by rods that were strong, must
be meant such rulers as were well qualified
for magistracy, such as had great abilities and
other qualifications fitting them for the business of rule. They were wont to choose a rod or
staff of the strongest and hardest sort of wood
that could be found, for the mace or sceptre of
a prince; such an one only being counted fit for
that use; and this generally was overlaid with
gold.

It is very remarkable that such a strong rod
should grow out of a weak vine: but so it had
been in Israel, through God's extraordinary
blessing, in times past. Though the nation is
spoken of here, and frequently elsewhere, as
weak and helpless in itself, and entirely depen-
dent as a vine, the weakest of all trees, that can-
not support itself by its own strength, and never
stands but as it leans on or hangs by something
else that is stronger than itself; yet God had
caused many of her sons to be strong rods fit for
sceptres; he had raised up in Israel many able
and excellent princes and magistrates, who had
done worthily in their day.

3. It should be understood and observed what is meant by these strong rods being broken and withered, *viz.* these able and excellent rulers being removed by death: men's dying is often compared in Scripture to the withering of the growth of the earth.

4. It should be observed after what manner the breaking and withering of these strong rods is here spoken of, *viz.* as a great and awful calamity, that God had brought upon that people: it is spoken of as one of the chief effects of God's dreadful displeasure against them; "But she was plucked up in fury, she was cast down to the ground, and the east wind dried up her fruit: her strong rods were broken and withered, the fire had consumed them." The great benefits she enjoyed while her strong rods remained, are represented in the preceding verse; "And she had strong rods for the scepters of them that bear rule, and her stature was exalted among the thick branches; and she appeared in her height with the multitude of her branches." And the terrible calamities that attended the breaking and withering of her strong rods, are represented in the two verses next following in the text; "And now she is planted in the wilderness, in a dry and thirsty ground. And fire is gone out of a rod of her branches, which hath devoured her fruit." And in the conclusion in the next words, is very emphatically declared the worthiness of such a dispensation to be greatly lamented; "So that she hath no strong

rod to be a scepter to rule: this is a lamentation, and shall be for a lamentation."

That which I therefore observe from the words of the text, to be the subject of discourse at this time, is this, *viz*. When God by death removes from a people those in place of public authority and rule that have been as strong rods, it is an awful judgment of God on that people, and worthy of great lamentation.

In discoursing on this proposition, I would,

1. Show what kind of rulers may fitly be called strong rods.

2. Show why the removal of such rulers from a people by death is to be looked upon as an awful judgment of God on that people, and is greatly to be lamented.

I. I would observe what qualifications of those who are in public authority and rule may properly give them the denomination of strong rods.

1. One qualification of rulers whence they may properly be denominated strong rods, is great ability for the management of public affairs. This is the case, when they who stand in a place of public authority are men of great natural abilities, men of uncommon strength of reason and largeness of understanding; especially when they have a remarkable genius for government, a peculiar turn of mind fitting them to gain an extraordinary understanding in things of that nature. They have ability, in

an especial manner, for insight into the mysteries of government, and for discerning those things wherein the public welfare or calamity consists, and the proper means to avoid the one and promote the other; an extraordinary talent at distinguishing what is right and just, from that which is wrong and unequal, and to see through the false colours with which injustice is often disguised, and unravel the false and subtle arguments and cunning sophistry that is often made use of to defend iniquity. They have not only great natural abilities in these respects, but their abilities and talents have been improved by study, learning, observation, and experience; and by these means they have obtained great actual knowledge. They have acquired great skill in public affairs, and things requisite to be known in order to their wise, prudent, and effectual management; they have obtained a great understanding of men and things, a great knowledge of human nature, and of the way of accommodating themselves to it, so as most effectually to influence it to wise purposes. They have obtained a very extensive knowledge of men with whom they are concerned in the management of public affairs, either those who have a joint concern in government, or those who are to be governed; and they have also obtained a very full and particular understanding of the state and circumstances of the country or people of whom they have the care, and know well their laws and constitution, and what their circumstances require; and likewise have a great knowledge of the people of neighboring nations, states, or provinces, with whom they have occasion to be concerned in the management of public affairs committed to them. These things all contribute to render those who are in authority fit to be denominated "strong rods."

2. When they have not only great understanding, but largeness of heart, and a greatness and nobleness of disposition, this is another qualification that belongs to the character of a "strong rod."

Those that are by Divine Providence set in a place of public authority and rule, are called "gods, and sons of the Most High," Psalm 82:6. And therefore it is peculiarly unbecoming them to be of a mean spirit, a disposition that will admit of their doing those things that are sordid and vile; as when they are persons of a narrow, private spirit, that may be found in little tricks and intrigues to promote their private interest. Such will shamefully defile their hands to gain a few pounds, are not ashamed to grind the faces of the poor, and screw their neighbours; and will take advantage of their authority or commission to line their own pockets with what is fraudulently taken or withheld from others. When a man in authority is of such a mean spirit, it weakens his authority, and makes him justly contemptible in the eyes of men, and is utterly inconsistent with his being a strong rod.

But on the contrary, it greatly establishes his authority, and causes others to stand in awe of him, when they see him to be a man of greatness of mind, one that abhors those things that are mean and sordid, and not capable of a compliance with them: one that is of a public spirit, and not of a private narrow disposition; a man of honour, and not of mean artifice and clandestine management, for filthy lucre; one that abhors trifling and impertinence, or to waste away his time, that should be spent in the service of God, his king, and his country, in vain amusements and diversions, and in the pursuit of the gratifications of sensual appetites. God charges the rulers in Israel, that pretended to be their great and mighty men, with being mighty to drink wine, and men of strength to mingle strong drink. There does not seem to be any reference to their being men of strong heads, and able to bear a great deal of strong drink, as some have supposed: there is a severe sarcasm in the words; for the prophet is speaking of the great men, princes, and judges in Israel (as appears by the verse next following,) which should be mighty men, strong rods, men of eminent qualifications, excelling in nobleness of spirit, of glorious strength and fortitude of mind; but instead of that, they were mighty or eminent for nothing but gluttony and drunkenness.

3. When those that are in authority are endowed with much of a spirit of government,

this is another thing that entitles them to the denomination of "strong rods." They not only are men of great understanding and wisdom in affairs that appertain to government, but have also a peculiar talent at using their knowledge, and exerting themselves in this great and important business, according to their great understanding in it. They are men of eminent fortitude, and are not afraid of the faces of men, are not afraid to do the part that properly belongs to them as rulers, though they meet with great opposition, and the spirits of men are greatly irritated by it. They have a spirit of resolution and activity, so as to keep the wheels of government in proper motion, and to cause judgment and justice to run down as a mighty stream; they have not only a great knowledge of government, and the things that belong to it in theory, but it is, as it were, natural to them to apply the various powers and faculties with which God has endowed them, and the knowledge they have obtained by study and observation, to that business, so as to perform it most advantageously and effectually.

4. Stability and firmness of integrity, fidelity, and piety, in the exercise of authority, is another thing that greatly contributes to, and is very essential in, the character of a "strong rod."

He is not only a man of strong reason and great discernment to know what is just, but is a man of strict integrity and righteousness, firm and immovable in the execution of justice and judgment. He is not only a man of great ability to bear down vice and immorality, but has a disposition agreeable to such ability; is one that has a strong aversion to wickedness, and is disposed to use the power God has put into his hands to suppress it; and is one that not only opposes vice by his authority, but by his example. He is one of inflexible fidelity, who will be faithful to God whose minister he is, to his people for good, and who is immovable in his regard to his supreme authority, his commands and his glory; and will be faithful to his king and country. He will not be induced by the many temptations that attend the business of men in public authority, basely to betray his trust; will not consent to do what he thinks not to be for the public good, for his own gain or advancement, or any private interest. He is well principled, and firm in acting agreeably to his principles, and will not be prevailed with to do otherwise through fear or favor, to follow a multitude, or to maintain his interest in any on whom he depends for the honor or profit of his place, whether it be prince or people; and is also one of that strength of mind, whereby he rules his own spirit. These things very eminently contribute to a ruler's title to the denomination of a "strong rod."

5. And *lastly*, It also contributes to that strength of a man in authority by which he may be denominated a "strong rod," when he is in

such circumstances as give him advantage for
the exercise of his strength for the public good;
as his being a person of honorable descent, of
a distinguished education, a man of estate, one
advanced in years, one that has long been in
authority, so that it is become as it were natural
for the people to pay him deference, to reverence
him, to be influenced and governed by him, and
to submit to his authority; and add to this, his
being extensively known, and much honoured
and regarded abroad; his being one of a good
presence, majesty of countenance, decency of
behavior, becoming one in authority; of forcible
speech, etc. These things add to his strength,
and increase his ability and advantage to serve
his generation in the place of a ruler, and therefore serve to render him one that is the more
fitly and eminently called a "strong rod."—I now
proceed,

II. To show that when such strong rods are
broken and withered by death, it is an awful
judgment of God on the people who are deprived
of them, and worthy of great lamentation.—And
that on two accounts.

1. By reason of the many positive benefits
and blessings to a people that such rulers are
the instruments of.

Almost all the prosperity of a public society
and civil community does, under God, depend
on their rulers. They are like the main springs
or wheels in a machine, that keep every part in
its due motion, and are in the body politic, as

the vitals in the body natural, and as the pillars and foundation in a building. Civil rulers are called "the foundations of the earth," Psalm 82 and 11:3.

The prosperity of a people depends more on their rulers than is commonly imagined. As they have the public society under their care and power, so they have advantage to promote the public interest every way; and if they are such rulers as have been described, they are some of the greatest blessings to the public. Their influence has a tendency to promote wealth, and cause temporal possessions and blessings to abound; and to promote virtue amongst them, and so unite them one to another in peace and mutual benevolence, and make them happy in society, each one the instrument of his neighbors' quietness, comfort, and prosperity; and by these means to advance their reputation and honour in the world; and which is much more, to promote their spiritual and eternal happiness. Therefore, the wise man says, Ecclesiastes 10:17. "Blessed art thou, O land, when thy king is the son of nobles."

We have a remarkable instance and evidence of the happy and great influence of such a strong rod as has been described, to promote the universal prosperity of a people, in the history of the reign of Solomon, though many of the people were uneasy under his government, and thought him too rigorous in his administrations: see 1 Kings 12:4. "Judah and Israel dwelt safely, every man under his vine and under his fig tree, from Dan even to Beersheba, all the days of Solomon." 1 Kings 4:25. "And he made silver to be among them as stones for abundance." Chapter 10:27. "And Judah and Israel were many, eating and drinking and making merry." [1 Kings 4:20]. The queen of Sheba admired, and was greatly affected with, the happiness of the people, under the government of such a strong rod, 1 Kings 10:8, 9. "Happy are thy men (says she), happy are these thy servants which stand continually before thee, and that hear thy wisdom. Blessed be the Lord thy God which delighted in thee, to set thee on the throne of Israel; because the Lord loved Israel for ever, therefore made he thee king, to do judgment and justice."

The flourishing state of the kingdom of Judah, while they had strong rods for the scepters of them that bare rule, is taken notice of in our context; "her stature was exalted among the thick branches, and she appeared in her height with the multitude of her branches."

Such rulers are eminently the ministers of God to his people for good: they are great gifts of the Most High to a people, blessed tokens of his favour, and vehicles of his goodness to them; and therein are images of his own Son, the grand medium of all God's goodness to fallen mankind; and therefore, all of them are called, sons of the Most High. All civil rulers, if they are as they ought to be, such strong rods as have been described, will be like the Son of the Most High, vehicles of good to mankind, and like him, will be as the light of the morning when the sun riseth, even a morning without clouds, as the tender grass springing out of the earth, by clear shining after rain. And therefore, when a people are bereaved of them, they sustain an unspeakable loss, and are the subjects of a judgment of God that is greatly to be lamented.

2. On account of the great calamities such rulers are a defense from. Innumerable are the grievous and fatal calamities which public societies are exposed to in this evil world, from which they can have no defense without order and authority. If a people are without government, they are like a city broken down and without walls, encompassed on every side by enemies, and become unavoidably subject to all manner of confusion and misery.

Government is necessary to defend communities from miseries from within themselves; from the prevalence of intestine discord, mutual injustice, and violence; the members of the society continually making a prey of one another, without any defense from each other. Rulers are the heads of union in public societies, that hold the parts together; without which nothing else is to be expected than that the members of the society will be continually divided against themselves, every one acting the part of an enemy to his neighbour, every one's hand against every man, and every man's hand against him; going on in remediless and endless broils and jarring, until the society be utterly dissolved and broken in pieces, and life itself, in the neighbourhood of our fellow-creatures, becomes miserable and intolerable.

We may see the need of government in societies by what is visible in families, those lesser societies, of which all public societies are constituted. How miserable would these little societies be, if all were left to themselves, without any authority or superiority in one above another, or any head of union and influence among them! We may be convinced by what we see of the lamentable consequences of the want of a proper exercise of authority and maintenance of government in families, which yet are not absolutely without all authority. No less need is there of government in public societies, but much more, as they are larger. A very few may possibly, without any government, act by concert, so as to concur in what shall be the welfare of the whole; but this is not to be expected among a multitude, constituted of many thousands, of a great variety of tempers and different interests.

As government is absolutely necessary, so there is a necessity of strong rods in order to it: the business being such as requires persons so qualified; no other being sufficient for, or well capable of, the government of public societies: and therefore, those public societies are miserable that have not such strong rods for sceptres to rule, Ecclesiastes 10:16."Woe to thee, O land, when thy king is a child."

As government, and strong rods for the exercise of it, are necessary to preserve public societies from dreadful and fatal calamities arising from among themselves; so no less requisite are they to defend the community from foreign enemies. As they are like the pillars of a building, so they are also like the walls and bulwarks of a city: they are under God the main strength of a people in the time of war, and the chief instruments of their preservation, safety, and rest. This is signified in a very lively manner in the words that are used by the Jewish community in her lamentations, to express the expectations she had from her princes, Lamentations 4:20. "The breath of our nostrils, the anointed of the Lord, was taken in their pits, of whom we said, Under his shadow we shall live among the heathen." In this respect also such strong rods are sons of the Most High, and images or resemblances of the Son of God, *viz.* as they are their saviours from their enemies; as the judges that God raised up of old in Israel are called, Nehemiah 9:27. "Therefore thou deliverest them into the hand of their enemies, who vexed them: and in the time of their trouble when they cried unto thee, thou heardest them from heaven; and according to thy manifold mercies, thou gavest them saviours, who saved them out of the hand of their enemies."

Thus both the prosperity and safety of a

people under God, depends on such rulers as are *strong rods*. While they enjoy such blessings, they are wont to be like a vine planted in a fruitful soil, with her stature exalted among the thick branches, appearing in her height with the multitude of her branches; but when they have no strong rod to be a sceptre to rule, they are like a vine planted in a wilderness that is exposed to be plucked up, and cast down to the ground, to have her fruit dried up with the east wind, and to have fire coming out of her own branches to devour her fruit.

On these accounts, when a people's strong rods are broken and withered, it is an awful judgment of God on that people, and worthy of great lamentation: as when king Josiah (who was doubtless one of the strong rods referred to in the text) was dead, the people made great lamentation for him, 2 Chronicles 35:24, 25. "And they brought him to Jerusalem, and he died, and was buried in one of the sepulchres of his fathers: and all Judah and Jerusalem mourned for Josiah. And Jeremiah lamented for Josiah: and all the singing-men and the singing-women spake of Josiah in their lamentations to this day, and made them an ordinance in Israel: and, behold, they are written in the lamentations."

APPLICATION

I come now to apply these things to our own case, under the late awful frown of Divine Providence upon us, in removing by death that honorable person in public rule and authority, an inhabitant of this town, and belonging to this congregation and church, who died at Boston the last Lord's day.

He was eminently a strong rod in the forementioned respects. As to his natural abilities, strength of reason, greatness and clearness of discerning, and depth of penetration, he was one of the first rank. It may be doubted whether he has left his superior in these respects in these parts of the world. He was a man of a truly great genius, and his genius was peculiarly fitted for the understanding and managing of public affairs.

And as his natural capacity was great, so was the knowledge that he had acquired, his understanding being greatly improved by close application of mind to those things he was called to be concerned in, and by a very exact observation of them, and long experience in them. He had indeed a great insight into the nature of public societies, the mysteries of government, and the affairs of peace and war. He had a discernment that very few have of those things wherein the public weal consists, and what those things are that expose public societies; and the proper means to avoid the latter, and promote the former. He was quick in his discerning, in that in most cases, especially such as belonged to his proper business, he at first sight would see further than most men when they had done their best; but yet he had a wonderful faculty of improving his own thoughts by meditation, and carrying his views a greater and greater length by long and close application of mind. He had an extraordinary ability to distinguish right and wrong, in the midst of intricacies, and circumstances that tended to perplex and darken the case. He was able to weigh things as it were in a balance, and to distinguish those things that were solid and weighty from those that had only a fair show without substance; which he evidently discovered in his accurate, clear, and plain way of stating and committing causes to a jury, from the bench, as by others hath been observed. He wonderfully distinguished truth from falsehood, and the most laboured cases seemed always to lie clear in his mind, his ideas being properly ranged; and he had a talent of communicating them to everyone's understanding, beyond almost any one; and if any were misguided, it was not because truth and falsehood, right and wrong, were not well distinguished.

He was probably one of the ablest politicians that ever New England bred. He had a very uncommon insight into human nature, and a marvellous ability to penetrate into particular tempers and dispositions of such as he had to deal with, and to discern the fittest way of treating them, so as most effectually to influence them to any good and wise purpose.

And never perhaps was there a person that had a more extensive and thorough knowledge of the state of this land, and its public affairs, and of persons that were jointly concerned with him in them. He knew this people, and their circumstances, and what their circumstances required. He discerned the diseases of this body, and what were the proper remedies, as an able and masterly physician. He had a great acquaintance with the neighbouring colonies, and also the nations on this continent, with whom we are concerned in our public affairs. He had a far greater knowledge than any other person in the land, of the several nations of Indians in these northern parts of America, their tempers, manners, and the proper way of treating them; and was more extensively known by them than any other person in the country. And no other person in authority in this province had such an acquaintance with the people and country of Canada, the land of our enemies, as he had.

He was exceeding far from a disposition and forwardness to intermeddle with other people's business; but as to what belonged to his proper business, in the offices he sustained, and the important affairs of which he had the care, he had a great understanding of what belonged to them. I have often been surprised at the length of his reach, and what I have seen of his ability to foresee and determine the consequences of things, even at a great distance, and quite beyond the sight of other men. He was not wavering and unsteady in his opinion. His manner was never to pass a judgment rashly, but was wont first thoroughly to deliberate and weigh an affair; and in this, notwithstanding his great abilities, he was glad to improve by the help of conversation and discourse with others, (and often spake of the great advantage he found by it,) but when, on mature consideration, he had settled his judgment, he was not easily turned from it by false colours, and plausible pretences and appearances.

And besides his knowledge of things belonging to his particular calling as a ruler, he had also a great degree of understanding in things belonging to his general calling as a Christian. He was no inconsiderable divine. He was a wise casuist, as I know by the great help I have found from time to time by his judgment and advice in cases of conscience, wherein I have consulted him. And indeed I scarce knew the divine that I ever found more able to help and enlighten the mind in such cases than he. And he had no small degree of knowledge in things pertaining to experimental religion; but was wont to discourse on such subjects, not only with accurate doctrinal distinctions, but as one intimately and feelingly acquainted with these things.

He was not only great in speculative knowledge, but his knowledge was practical; such as tended to a wise conduct in the affairs, business, and duties of life; so as properly to have the denomination of wisdom, and so as properly and eminently to invest him with the character of a wise man. And he was not only eminently wise and prudent in his own conduct, but was

one of the ablest and wisest counselors of others
in any difficult affair.

The greatness and honourableness of his
disposition was answerable to the largeness of
his understanding. He was naturally of a great
mind; in this respect he was truly the son of
nobles. He greatly abhorred things which were
mean and sordid, and seemed to be incapable of
a compliance with them. How far was he from
trifling and impertinence in his conversation!
How far from a busy, meddling disposition!
How far from any sly and clandestine management to fill his pockets with what was fraudulently withheld, or violently squeezed, from the
labourer, soldier, or inferior officer! How far
from taking advantage from his commission or
authority, or any superior power he had in his
hands; or the ignorance, dependence, or necessi-
ties of others; to add to his own gains with what
properly belonged to them, and with what they
might justly expect as a proper reward for any
of their services! How far was he from secretly
taking bribes offered to induce him to favour
any man in his cause, or by his power or interest to promote his being advanced to any place
of public trust, honour, or profit! How greatly
did he abhor lying and prevarication! And how
immovably steadfast was he to exact truth! His
hatred of those things that were mean and sordid was so apparent and well known, that it
was evident that men dreaded to appear in any
thing of that nature in his presence.

He was a man of a remarkably public spirit, a true lover of his country, and who greatly abhorred sacrificing the public welfare to private interest.—He was very eminently endowed with a spirit of government. The God of nature seemed to have formed him for government, as though he had been made on purpose, and cast into a mold, by which he should be every way fitted for the business of a man in public authority. Such a behaviour and conduct was natural to him, as tended to maintain his authority, and possess others with awe and reverence, and to enforce and render effectual what he said and did in the exercise of his authority. He did not bear the sword in vain: he was truly a terror to evil-doers. What I saw in him often put me in mind of that saying of the wise man, Proverbs 20:8. "The king that sitteth in the throne of judgment scattereth away all evil with his eyes." He was one that was not afraid of the faces of men; and every one knew that it was in vain to attempt to deter him from doing what, on mature consideration, he had determined he ought to do.— Every thing in him was great, and becoming a man in his public station. Perhaps never was there a man that appeared in New England to whom the denomination of *a great man* did more properly belong.

But though he was one that was great among men, exalted above others in abilities and greatness of mind, and in the place of rule, and feared not the faces of men, yet he feared God. He was strictly conscientious in his conduct, both in public and private. I never knew the man that seemed more steadfastly and immovably to act by principle, and according to rules and maxims, established and settled in his mind by the dictates of his judgment and conscience. He was a man of strict justice and fidelity. Faithfulness was eminently his character. Some of his greatest opponents that have been of the contrary party to him in public affairs, yet have openly acknowledged this of him, that he was a faithful man. He was remarkably faithful in his public trusts. He would not basely betray his trust, from fear or favour. It was in vain to expect it; however men might oppose him or neglect him, and how great soever they were: nor would he neglect the public interest committed to him, for the sake of his own ease, but diligently and laboriously watched and laboured for it night and day. And he was faithful in private affairs as well as public. He was a most faithful friend; faithful to any one that in any case asked his counsel: and his fidelity might be depended upon in whatever affair he undertook for any of his neighbours.

He was a noted instance of the virtue of temperance, unalterable in it, in all places, in all companies, and in the midst of all temptations. Though he was a man of a great spirit, yet he had a remarkable government of his spirit; and excelled in the government of his tongue. In the midst of all provocations from multitudes he

had to deal with, and the great multiplicity of
perplexing affairs in which he was concerned,
and all the opposition and reproaches of which
he was at any time the subject; yet what was
there that ever proceeded out of his mouth that
his enemies could lay hold of? No profane lan-
guage, no vain, rash, unseemly, and unchristian
speeches. If at any time he expressed himself
with great warmth and vigour, it seemed to be
from principle and determination of judgment,
rather than from passion. When he expressed
himself strongly, and with vehemence, those
that were acquainted with him, and well
observed him from time to time, might evidently
see it was done in consequence of thought and
judgment, weighing the circumstances and consequences of things.

The calmness and steadiness of his behavior
in private, particularly in his family, appeared
remarkable and exemplary to those who had
most opportunity to observe. He was thoroughly
established in those religious principles and
doctrines of the first fathers of New England,
usually called the *doctrines of grace,* and had
a great detestation of the opposite errors of
the present fashionable divinity, as very contrary to the word of God, and the experience of
every true Christian. And as he was a friend to
truth, so he was a friend to vital piety and the
power of godliness, and every countenanced and
favoured it on all occasions.

He abhorred profaneness, and was a person

of a serious and decent spirit, and ever treated sacred things with reverence. He was exemplary for his decent attendance on the public worship of God. Who ever saw him irreverently and indecently lolling, and laying down his head to sleep, or gazing about the meeting-house in time of divine service? And as he was able (as was before observed) to discourse very understandingly of experimental religion, so to some persons with whom he was very intimate, he gave intimations sufficiently plain, while conversing on these things, that they were matters of his own experience. And some serious persons in civil authority, who have ordinarily differed from him in matters of government, yet on some occasional close conversation with him on things of religion, have manifested a high opinion of him as to real experimental piety.

As he was known to be a serious person, and an enemy to a profane or vain conversation, so he was feared on that account by great and small. When he was in the room, only his presence was sufficient to maintain decency; though many were there accounted great men, who otherwise were disposed to take a much greater freedom in their talk and behaviour, than they dared to do in his presence. He was not unmindful of death, nor insensible of his own frailty, nor did death come unexpected to him. For some years past, he has spoken much to some persons of dying, and going to the eternal world, signifying that he did not expect to continue long here.

Added to all these things, to render him eminently a *strong rod*, he was attended with many circumstances which tended to give him advantage for the exerting of his strength for the public good. He was honorably descended, was a man of considerable substance, had been long in authority, was extensively known and honoured abroad, was high in the esteem of the many tribes of Indians in the neighbourhood of the British colonies, and so had great influence upon them above any other man in New England. God had endowed him with a comely presence, and majesty of countenance, becoming the great qualities of his mind, and the place in which God had set him.

In the exercise of these qualities and endowments, under these advantages, he has been as it were a father to this part of the land, on whom the whole county had, under God, its dependence in all its public affairs, and especially since the beginning of the present war. How much the weight of all the warlike concerns of the country (which above any part of the land lies exposed to the enemy) has lain on his shoulders, and how he has been the spring of all motion, and the doer of every thing that has been done, and how wisely and faithfully he has conducted these affairs, I need not inform this congregation. You well know that he took care of the county as a father of a family of children, not neglecting men's lives, and making light of their blood; but with great diligence, vigilance, and prudence, applying himself continually to the proper means of our safety and welfare. And especially has this his native town, where he has dwelt from his infancy, reaped the benefit of his happy influence. His wisdom has been, under God, very much our guide, and his authority our support and strength, and he has been a great honour to Northampton, and ornament to our church. He continued in full capacity of usefulness while he lived; he was indeed considerably advanced in years, but his powers of mind were not sensibly abated, and his strength of body was not so impaired, but that he was able to go on long journeys, in extreme heat and cold, and in a short time.

But now this "strong rod is broken and withered," and surely the judgment of God therein is very awful, and the dispensation that which may well be for a lamentation. Probably we shall be more sensible of the worth and importance of such a strong rod by the want of it. The awful voice of God in this providence is worthy to be attended to by this whole province, and especially by the people of this county, but in a more peculiar manner by us of this town. We have now this testimony of the divine displeasure, added to all the other dark clouds God has lately brought over us, and his awful frowns upon us. It is a dispensation, on many accounts, greatly calling for our humiliation and fear before God; an awful manifestation of his supreme, universal, and absolute dominion, calling us to adore

the divine sovereignty, and tremble at the presence of this great God. And it is a lively instance
of human frailty and mortality. We see how that
none are out of the reach of death, that no greatness, no authority, no wisdom and sagacity, no
honourableness of person or station, no degree
of valuableness and importance, exempts from
the stroke of death. This is therefore a loud and
solemn warning to all sorts to prepare for their
departure hence.

And the memory of this person who is now
gone, who was made so great a blessing while
he lived, should engage us to show respect and
kindness to his family. This we should do both
out of respect to him and to his father, your former eminent pastor, who in his day was in a
remarkable manner a father to this part of the
land in spirituals, and especially to this town,
as this his son has been in temporals.—God
greatly resented it, when the children of Israel
did not show kindness to the house of Jerubbaal
that had been made an instrument of so much
good to them, Judges 8:35. "Neither showed they
kindness to the house of Jerubbaal, according to
all the good which he had showed unto Israel."

NOTES

NOTES

NOTES

MAN'S QUESTIONS & GOD'S ANSWERS

Am I accountable to God?
"Every one of us shall give account of himself to God." (Romans 14:12).

Has God seen all my ways?
"All things are naked and opened unto the eyes of Him with whom we have to do." (Hebrews 4:13).

Does He charge me with sin?
"The Scripture hath concluded all under sin." (Galatians 3:22).
"All have sinned." (Romans 3:23).

Will He punish sin?
"The soul that sinneth, it shall die." (Ezekiel 18:4).
"For the wages of sin is death." (Romans 6:23).

Must I perish?
"God is not willing that any perish, but that all should come to repentance." (2 Peter 3:9).

How can I escape?
"Believe on the Lord Jesus Christ, and thou shalt be saved." (Acts 16:31).

Is He able to save me?
"He is able also to save them to the uttermost that come unto God by Him." (Hebrews 7:25).

Is He willing?
"Christ Jesus came into the world to save sinners." (1 Timothy 1:15).

Am I saved on believing?
"He that believeth on the Son hath everlasting life." (John 3:36).

Can I be saved now?
"Now is the accepted time; behold, now is the day of salvation." (2 Corinthians 6:2).

As I am?
"Him that cometh to Me I will in no wise cast out." (John 6:37).

Shall I not fall away?
"Him that is able to keep you from falling." (Jude 24).

If saved, how should I live?
"They which live should not henceforth live unto themselves, but unto Him which died for them." (2 Corinthians 5:15).

What about death, and eternity?
"I go to prepare a place for you; that where I am, there ye may be also." (John 14:2, 3).